Psychoanalysis

Violence in children, adolescents, adults and supervision

Athina Alexandris, M.D.
Psyhcoanalyst, member of I.P.A.

Paschalidis Medical Publications

Notice

Medicine is an ever-changing science. As new research and clinical experiences broaden our knowledge, changes in treatment and drug therapy are required. The editor and the publisher of this work have checked with sources believed to be reliable in their efforts to provide information that is complete and generally in accord with the standards accepted at the time of publication. However, in view of the possibility of human error or changes in medical sciences, neither the editor nor the publisher nor any other party who has been involved in the preparation of publication of this work warrants that the information contained herein is in every respect accurate or complete, and they disclaim all responsibility for any errors or omissions or for the results obtained from use of the information contained in this work. Readers are encouraged to confirm the information contained herein with other sources. For example and in particular, readers are advised to check the product information sheet included in the package of each drug they plan to administer to be certain that the information contained in this work is accurate and that changes have not been made in the recommended dose or in the contraindications for administration. This recommendation is of particular importance in connection with new or infrequently used drugs.

ISBN: 978-960-399-659-0

9 789603 996590

14th, Tetrapoleos str., Athens, 115 27, Greece
Tel.: 003-210-7789125, 003-210-7793012, Fax: 003-210-7759421,
e-mail:
orders: Paschalidis@Medical-Books.gr
© information: GP@Medical-Books.gr, CP@Medical-Books.gr

Acknowledgment

I am grateful to all those who provided me with the moral and material support necessary to achieve my goals. They enabled me pursue my studies at medical school at the University of Athens and to specialise abroad at McGill University and at the Canadian Institute of Psychoanalysis, where I also taught afterwards during my years in Canada.

Thanks are likewise due to Professor of Pediatrics and Academician Nikolaos Matsaniotis who gave me the opportunity of teaching and practising child psychiatry for many years at the Ayia Sophia Children's Hospital of the University of Athens. This is the hospital in which I trained in pediatrics under Professor C. Horemis and where I had the occasion to make the acquaintance of Professor Matsaniotis, who supported me greatly in my new speciality of child psychiatry and child analysis upon my return to Greece.

I am particularly grateful to Dr Costas N. Stefanis, Professor of Psychiatry and President of the Academy of Athens, who, when I returned to Athens, gave me the opportunity to teach in the University of Athens Department of Psychiatry for some 30 years under his chairmanship. I taught theory of psychoanalysis and supervision of psychiatrists.

I would also like to acknowledge that the experience of teaching contributed greatly to my professional and personal growth.

INDRODUCTION

This monograph consists of two parts. The first has to do with the supervision of analysts on an individual basis, and with the group supervision of psychiatrists and psychologists. The group supervision presented here is one of several that took place at the University of Athens Department of Psychiatry, where I taught for many years under the chairmanship of Professor Costas N. Stefanis.

The second part consists of individual cases selected from my private practice. The criterion for selecting these cases was that they revolved around the same themes - violence and its derivatives - as the supervisions in part one of the monograph.

It goes without saying that the content of this monograph is part of my preoccupation with my profession. What motivated me to write about this was the notion of gaining greater insight into these matters. The writing has in fact has helped me greatly. It is my hope that this monograph will prove useful to analysts and related professionals.

CONTENTS

A

SUPERVISION

1. Attacks on the mind, attacks on linking in individual and group supervision

2. Moments of supervision: 1. 2. 3. 4. 5.

1. Attacks on the mind, attacks on linking in individual and group supervision*

On chereche l' inconnu
Et au fond de l' inconnu
Pour trouver du nouveau
Charles Baudelaire
1821-1867

Abstract

The purpose of this paper, which is based on the theories of Freud, Klein, and Bion, is to describe the destructive attacks of a patient on the state of mind and on the linking function of her therapist during both individual and group supervision. In both cases, the patient succeeded in fulfilling her wish to destroy the link between objects and ultimately to be rejected.

Such attacks are initiated by emotions and motivated by hate and envy, as described by Freud (1911, 1920), supplemented and expanded by Klein (1928-1957), and by Bion (1955-1985).

Bion (1962) says that, in an attempt "to understand our understanding, we meet with obscurity". Clinical experience has led me to believe that the obscurity regarding the attacks is related, among other factors, to the very nature of the unconscious wish that is pressing for fulfillment. This view will be investigated further.

The nature of the unconscious link between patient and analyst will also be discussed, as will some of the dynamics of the group.

* Presended at the 1st Europian conference on Psycho therapy, 11-14, Sept. 1997.

Introduction

According to Bion, "destructive attacks are made when the main failure takes place at the point which Klein describes as the development of the depressive position: When the infant would become aware of his relationship with whole objects, and thereby of the feelings of depression and guilt associated with the depressive position. It is at this point however that the patient or the patient's id makes destructive attacks on all those aspects of his personality, his ego, that are concerned with establishing external and internal contact". He goes on (1955) to say that the attacks "are all true examples of the mechanisms described by Klein (1930, 1948-1957) in her discussion of the paranoid and depressive position and particularly of projective identification". While she goes on to describe the child's fantasized sadistic attacks on the mother's body (and its contents), Bion (1962) expanded her views by saying that these attacks are against the ego, which he calls "castration of the ego", and that the sadistic attacks are also on verbal thought which causes the splitting that Freud and others have described. Bion's (1955) view is that this "splitting of verbal thought is carried out cruelly and the attempts at synthesis which are typical of the depressive position are frustrated because the splits are brought together cruelly".

Bion uses the term "link" in two ways: first, "as whatever links one object to another"; and second, link as the patient's "relationship with a function that subserves a function of providing the link between two objects". He speaks "of the destructive attacks the patient makes on anything which is felt to have the function of linking one object with another". Bion says that, "fantasized attacks on the breast are the prototype of all attacks on objects that serve as a link and projective identification is the mechanism employed by the psyche to dispose of the ago fragments produced by its destructiveness". "Excessive destructiveness commences with life itself... And internal or external objects are in fact part objects... in this state of mind, emotion is hated; it is felt to be too powerful to be contained by the immature psyche. It is felt to link objects and it gives reality to objects which are not self and therefore inimical to primary narcissism. These attacks on the linking function of emotion lead to an over-prominence of links which appear to be logical but are never emotionally reasonable. Consequently the links surviving are perverse, cruel and sterile" Bion, 1959. "The patient could make destructive attacks by his" conduct designed to destroy whatever links the two objects "analyst - analysand, such as stammer, sleep, lack of dreams, silences, etc." Bion 1959.

Supervision

A psychiatrist who was a participant in the group I supervised asked for an individual supervision from me. He said he was distressed because things had ended very badly with a patient of his. A woman in her early thirties asked him for an urgent consultation following the death of a female relative from cancer. She had taken care of this sick person whose demands she felt had drained her. The patient herself had a mastectomy some years previously and had been well since then.

She was in a terrified and furious state; she was afraid that she would have a recurrence of cancer. Her speech resembled the burst of a machine gum with stops in between. Her sentences were unfinished; her thoughts disconnected and disjointed.

The supervisee read me the session which he had written. When we discussed the case, I observed that he was unable to make a synthesis and that he omitted parts of the clinical material which he himself had written in his report and had just read. Then I asked him to read the report again, and we discussed the case once more. The same phenomenon occurred. The clinical material which he had omitted was evidence of the patient's severe disturbance, namely that her head buzzed and her thoughts were like flies circling around inside her head. This could be understood as the turmoil of her internal part objects, as Bion's bizarre objects or Bion's "thoughts without a thinker". The patient had said that significant persons in her life "pierce me with their eyes, and I feel that they are draining me. My boyfriend bewitched me with his eyes, he reads my thoughts. I' m afraid that he will drive me crazy. I am losing my independence, my foundation. In the beginning, I liked him very much, but as time went on, I began to lose control of the situation. I decided not to see him again. I stopped working and this wiped me out completely. I don't want to have feelings, not dependencies. I want you to tell me what to do". The supervisee who is a kind and gentle person, tried to pacify her, prescribed some medication and made a further appointment to see her. However, the patient cancelled her appointment by telephoning him, accusing him of all sorts of things, including incompetence as a doctor. The supervisee was unable to respond to this telephone call and allowed her to leave, thus satisfying her unconscious wish to be rejected. He felt frustrated, ashamed and guilty that he had not been more competent and able to keep the patient in treatment.

So what did happen to this competent psychiatrist? His mind was attacked by the patient. He could not think and his patient had caused him cruel splitting which prevented him from being able to make an integration, a synthesis of the clinical material, in other words, his ego functions. His attention, memory, judgement, etc., had been attacked, as described by Freud (1911). Bion (1955) said that the "attack on the ego is identical with the destructive attacks of the patient or the patient's id on verbal thought which is inevitably an attack on all". The supervisee' linking function was also attacked by the cruel splitting, and that is why during our discussion he had omitted parts of the clinical material which he had just read. In addition, the patient put the doctor in the role of satisfying her wish to be rejected, employing the mechanism of projective identification and counter-identification (Grinberg 1956-1993). The patient's capacity for linkage seemed to be limited and the links which she used to link with objects appeared to be cruel and over prominent.

The link between patient and doctor was shaken, maybe damaged, but not totally destroyed. It is interesting to note that the supervise, on his own initiative, called the patient two weeks later to find out how she was. The patient also called him a few times over the next six months, continuing her threats and accusations against him. They never met again.

The patient, attacked and abandoned the doctor, but she left something behind her: she mobilized his feelings. She motivated him to ask for supervision so that he could learn more about her.

Group supervision
(the group consists of psychiatrists and psychologists)

My supervisee and I decided, at the end of this supervision, to present this case to an ongoing group in which he was a participant and I was the supervisor. This was a working group motivated to search for the truth, the unconscious.

When the supervisee presented the case to the group, the same phenomena were observed as those in the individual supervision, i.e. the patient attacked the mind of the group in the same way she had attacked her doctor. She caused cruel splitting on their minds, and the inability to integrate and make a synthesis of the clinical material. During the discussion, it became evident that the group omitted the same clinical material that the patient's doctor had omitted in the individual supervision.

The linking between objects - the participants - was also attacked by the patient. During the discussion, the participants gave the impression that they were functioning like the flies in the patient's head, like Bion's bizarre objects. The participants were not listening nor responding to each other; they gave no evidence of being affected by what was said. The end result was the patient's rejection by the group as untreatable, unalysable, unpleasant, and unbearable. That is, the group, too, fulfilled her wish to be rejected.

After listening to the case presentation, the group at first reacted with silence. Then they began to ask irrelevant questions, after which they started attacking the presenter of the case, making derogative remarks about him. As the group was gradually becoming aggressive, I had to intervene to, protect the presenter. The tension was mounting and the time devoted to the supervision was coming to an end. At this point I decided to offer them the understanding of the case, by integrating the clinical material, bringing to the fore transference and counter transference issues etc., thinking that it would satisfy them and therefore relieve their tension.

During the coffee break which followed the supervision, several members of the group attacked both the presenter of the case and the supervisor (myself), gossiping and belittling both of us, as I was told afterwards by members of the group.

The group's comments upset me greatly. I felt they were being unfair to me. Then I was attacked by my own super - ego, feeling shame and guilt for not being a more competent supervisor. However, all these attacks made by the patient against the supervise and the group and finally against me, motivated me to investigate further what had gone wrong during the supervision.

Evidently, the group, instead of behaving as a "work group", changed to the more regressive basic assumption of "fight-flight", attacking its leader as a kind of counter-projective identification reaction to the patient's pathological projective identifications. In response, the group made a counter - attack against the patient to the point of total rejection. The supervisor was protected during the time of the supervision by the group due to the split of the object and its mechanism. So what I should have done was to deal first with the affect of the group (Kernberg 1996), help the participants to pass from the schizoid state to the depressive position satisfying thus their anaclytic needs, before attempting to satisfy their need to understand the unknown the case which belongs to the depressive position.

My intervention, i.e. the formulation with reference to the understanding of the case, caused more frustration and provoked envy and hatred towards myself, the supervisor. Hate begets hate and frustration begets frustration. The group acted out their feelings toward me in my absence during the coffee break. It is possible that the group felt "derision en mirror" as described by Anzieu" (1981). Also, the group might have felt that my intervention was intended to force them to pass abruptly from the schizoid to the depressive position which causes fear of emotional explosion, or that I ignored their emotional state.

The link between the group and the supervisor was shaken but not destroyed, and we continued our work for another year. In other works, the group managed to survive the destructiveness of the patient and its consequences.

I was tempted to present the same case by the same presenter to another group I was supervising at that time, as I wanted to see their reaction. Sure enough, the same phenomena described above were repeated.

Obscurity related to the nature of the desire

Clinical experience has led me to believe that the obscurity regarding the understanding of the patient's attacks is related, among other factors, to the nature of the unconscious wish pressing for fulfillment. This is evident in the case presented above. The patient's wish to be cared for is obscured by her attacks, threats and accusations, so that her desire is not recognized nor manifested either to others or even to herself. Her need to be punished for having such a desire further obscures the picture and leads to the confusion of internal and external communication. This obscurity is inherent in various cases, e.g. there are patients who fear hate and envy to the extent that steps are taken to destroy awareness of all feelings, especially those of desire. Other patients are often looking for an accomplice or for someone to whom they can assign the role of fulfilling their wish. This is another way to obscure the wish as well as the communication between subject and object.

Not infrequently there are cases of patients who have feelings and sensations they cannot learn from; the are equally incapable of knowing the meaning of these feelings. Bion says, "No desire, no memory". Freud (1911) describes patients who have not "learned or comprehended the qualities ... of pleasure or pain". An analysand of mine asked me: "Is there a feeling in me? Whatever it is, it is something anonymous, not even a sound, and if I try to describe the undescribable, will this undescribable thing come out? How long will it take? How many years will I have to go on trying?" Or like Joyce McDougall's case (1997) who had "no desires because she was never desired". We could go on citing examples from the analytical practice of other analysts or from my own. In the above cases there is a common factor related to the nature of the wish seeking fulfillment the various forms of acting out. That is, attack as a form of communication, as a link, as a need to find a container with a capacity of "reverie", as an evacuation of the aggressive parts of the self, or aggressive internal objects, in order to get rid of them, or as the manifestation of the destructive aspect of a psychotic personality, attack as a defense to avoid anxiety or pain, as an escape from fear of envy either his own or from others (Bion 1962); attacks employed to cover up or deny a desire, attacks aiming at the discovery of a desire, attack as a plea for help.

Thoughts on the unconscious link between analyst - analysand

The nature of the unconscious link between analyst - analysand is under constant study by several contemporary theoreticians. It covers themes such as the transitional field joining the unconscious of the analyst and the unconscious of the analysand (Frayn 1993); the inter subjective field of the "analytical third" by Ogden (1994), or unconscious fantasies and reveries; also similarities between the two parties involved, etc. However, it is beyond the scope of this paper to review the literature on this subject. My intention is to note some factors which in my experience seem to favor the analytical process: above all, the truthfulness of the relationship between the two parties, the capacity of the analyst to contain the unknown parts of both the analysand and his own personality; also, the capacity to establish and maintain the linkage between the two parties in question. It is possible that the nature of the unconscious link between the analyst and the analysand is affected by similarities in their "undigested facts" (Bion) 1962.

And last, but not least, is the "libidinal investment" in the relationship by both parties, as beautifully described by Joyce McDougall in "Many Faces of Errors" (1995), and in her fascinating article "Somatic Violence and the Therapeutic Relationship" (1997). I am in agreement with her opinion that it is easier for an analyst to speak about hate and envy than to speak about loving feeling and the libidinal bond which develops between the two parties concerned. Taking into consideration the fact that the motive in the psychic process is a wish to be fulfilled, the analyst's wish is to seek to understand the unconscious which corresponds to "un voeu tres profond" Anzieu (1981). It is wish that brings us together in this conference.

In conclusion, analysts are motivated by their patients' destructive attacks and may only continue to search for the unknown "in order to achieve new understandings and open new questions most often without an answer, thus expanding the infinite area of what is knowable/unknowable", as Bion says (1962).

REFERENCES

Anzieu, D. (1975): Le groupe et l' inconsient L' imaginaire groupal. Paris: Dumod.

Bion, W.R. (1955): Language and the schizophrenic. In: M. Klein, P. Heimann, R.E. Money-Kyrle (eds): New Directions in Psychoanalysis. London: Tavistock (Reprinted London: Karnac Books, 1977).

Bion, W.R. (1957): The differentiation of the psychotic from the non-psychotic part of the personality. International Journal of Psychoanalysis, vol. 38, parts 3-4. Reprinted in: Second Thoughts, pp. 43-64.

Bion, W.R. (1959): Attacks on linking. International Journal of Psychoanalysis, vol 40, parts 5-6. Reprinted in: Second Thoughts: selected papers on psychoanalysis, (1967), pp. 93-109, London: Maresfield.

Bion, W.R. (1962): Learning from experience. London: Heinemann. (Reprinted: London, Karnac Books, 19).

Frayn, D.H. (1993): Influence of dyadic factors on enactment. Canadian Journal of Psychoanalysis, vol. 2, 61-83.

Freud, S. (1911): Formulations regarding the two principles of mental functioning. S.E.

Grinberg, L. (1993): Counter transference and projective counter - identification. In: Alexandris A., Vaslamatzis G., (eds): Counter transference, London: Karnac Books.

Grinberg, L., Sor, D., ...abak de Bianchedi, E. (1993): New Introduction to the Work of Bion, rev. ed., Northvale: Jason Aronson.

Kernberg, O. (1996): 26-28 July, 4th Int. Psych symposium Delphi: (The concern of Libido in the light of contemporary Psycho - Theorizing).

Klein, M. (1935): A contribution to the psychogenesis of manic - depressive states. In: The Writings of Melanie Klein, vol. I: Love, Guilt and Reparation, London: Hogarth Press.

Mc Dougall, J. (1997): Somatic violence and the therapeutic relationship. Canadian Journal of Psychoanalysis, vol. 5, 53-60.

Mc Dougall, J. (1995): The many faces of Eros. New York: WW. Norton.

Ogden, 1. (1994): The analytic third - working with inter subjective clinical facts. International Journal of Psychoanalysis, 75:3-20.

2. Moments of supervision

1. An experienced analyst came to supervision in an effort to understand the nightmares that both he and his analysand had had the night of a cancelled appointment. The supervisor - myself, after listening to what the supervisee had to say, pointed out what had escaped his attention, i.e. that the regular, planned sessions - meeting each other - (analyst-analysand) kept both their ghosts under control. In other words, the defensive role played by the sessions - or "meetings" together - was explained to the supervisee. The cancellation of one meeting was enough to lift the "censorship" of the defences and to produce nightmares in both parties. In addition, the cancellation of the appointment - that is not seeing each other - was the day residue of the nightmares of both analyst and analysand. The supervisee accepted my view with some reluctance and shame, but finally he accepted his own particular problem and understood that he had to work it out in order to become more effective in his profession. It is the supervisor's opinion that the analyst's motivation for seeking supervision was concern about his effectiveness as a psychoanalyst in this particular case.

2. Simultaneous regression of analyst and his analysand due to a common "traumatic" experience of unrequited love when they were both young men. More specifically, the supervisee reported to his supervisor that his analysand brought him a dream about an "unrequited love" that he had had as a young man. The analysand is now a middle-aged married man with children.

The same night, the analyst, also a middle-aged married man, had a dream identical to that which was reported to him by his analysand, i.e. he too dreamed about an "unrequited love" when he was a young man.

In this particular supervision, the supervisee was marginally aware of the simultaneous regression of himself and his analysand. It is worth noting that the supervisee became very upset at his own dream of unrequited love that had come to visit and remind him that the case was not closed.

On the other hand, it gave him the opportunity to work out his regression and his identification with the analysand more fully and eventually to become more skilled in his profession.

3. My supervisee's analysand, a physician who works in the intensive care unit of a hospital, mobilised archaic fears in his analyst to the degree that she became panicky and sought supervision urgently because she believed that her analysand was performing euthanasia selectively on his patients in the ICU instead of treating them. The supervisor received an analyst in a state of panic. However the clinical material and the dreams of the analysand that she brought to supervision by no means supported the supervisee's view. This is an example of a very intelligent and gifted analyst whose own unresolved problems were interfering with her profession.

The supervisor very tactfully told the supervisee that she did not share the latter's view about the analysand and that the supervisee was over-reacting. Then the supervisee went on to say that there were some extreme events taking place in her own family that indicated that euthanasia had been performed. The supervisee was helped to understand what this particular analysand symbolised for her, and her panic was reduced.

4. An analyst came for supervision because he had a panic attack after being seduced by his analysand. He stated that he was unable to continue the analysis with this particular analysand and was considering finding some pretext for referring him to another analyst, because he could neither deal with his panic nor understand it.

During the supervision, it became evident that my supervisee was aware of his panic but not of its homosexual nature. It also became clear that his analysand throughout analysis was attempting to seduce him, by various means, saying e.g. that he was impotent, that he was not interested in girls, etc., but the analyst denied the seductive behaviour.

What broke down the analyst's denial was the dream which his analysand reported to him, in which the latter performed anal intercourse on a man.

Thus the panic attack of my supervisee was triggered by his

analysand's dream. The analyst was now unconsciously in panic that his analysand would express his homosexual feelings towards him directly, i.e. to make advances to him.

The supervisor shared her thoughts with the supervisee and suggested that he should work through his latent homosexuality. The supervisee was hesitant but eventually accepted the suggestion offered by his supervisor.

5. A 40-year-old group therapist came for supervision because she felt that she was unable to handle her group during the last session, and felt powerless and helpless. She stated the group took over her role.

What emerged from the content of the session that she presented to the supervisor was that she was sinking in the psychic pain of the group whose therapy she was conducting, and in this way lost control of the group.

But let us take things from the beginning. When this skilled, well- trained and analysed group therapist entered my office and sat down, I noticed that she was not her usual self. She looked ill, pale, and scruffy. She was not made up; her hair had not been combed. I asked her if anything was wrong with her, she said no. But she failed to convince me. She went on to present the group session. The first to speak, a male member of the group, who eventually became the protagonist, reported that since childhood he had been suffering from intense psychic pain and that he was trapped within it, not knowing what to do. He went on to say that his mother as well was trapped in her own intense psychic pain. When these feelings became unbearable, she ended up banging her head on the wall until she collapsed. Obviously she was unable to find an outlet. The only thing that the group as a whole, including the therapist, could do was to console the protagonist and feel pity for him, i.e. they could offer him no solution.

My estimation was that the protagonist had managed to drown and trap the entire group in his psychic pain because the group identified with him and his pain. The therapist also identified with the protagonist and, through him, with his mother. I pointed out this dynamic phenomenon to my supervisee. She confirmed my view and broke into tears. She said that for personal reasons she, too, was trapped in her own psychic pain and that so far she had been unable to work it out.

Her confession confirmed the supervisor's first impression of the group therapist, i.e. that something very serious was going on in her life.

The above incident raises the question of what an analyst or therapist should do in such painful situations or in even more serious ones involving the death of a loved one.

Each of us should do the best for our analysands, for our professional activities and for ourselves.

Often an analyst finds it necessary to postpone or cancel some or all of his or her analytic work and resume it when he feels ready to reassume his professional activities.

B

CASES SELECTED: 8 CASES

1. Violent memory: warning of imminent suicide: 4 cases

2. Violence in cases of adults: 4 cases

1. Violent memory: warning of imminent suicide: 4 cases*

Abstract

This paper is mainly based on the work of Sigmund Freud, E. Jakobson, O. Kernberg, M. Mahler and D.W. Winnicott. The intention is to demonstrate, through the presentation of clinical material, that violent memory should be considered first as a warning signal of imminent suicide.

Secondly, it should be seen as a scream for help, requiring that measures be taken to prevent suicidal modes of life and, of course, the act itself.

In the case of psychoanalysis, the analyst defends life by working through the violent memory as thoroughly as possible in each particular case. It is suggested that the analyst must be cautious and above all, that violence not be met with violence, since working through is played out in the transference-countertransference arena.

Violent memory - affective memory - is related to severe traumatic experiences in early life rather than to psychiatric diagnostic categories.

My experience has led me to agree with Kernberg's view that affective memory "... is built up in the undifferentiated symbiotic phase in the context of infant-mother interactions ...". This view will be investigated further.

The other side of the violent memory coin is that it could also be a signal of imminent murder. This will not be dealt with here, even though it came out in the clinical material, as it is beyond the scope of this conference.

* This paper was presented at 20th congress of the international Association for suicidal prevention, Held i Athens, Greece 1999.

Introduction

The purpose of this presentation is to share experience, to broaden understanding and hopefully to improve our therapeutic techniques in relation to those subjects who are tormented by the violence of memory.

For this presentation, violent memory is defined as the memory of a violent affect e.g. "*My memory of myself is terror*". This memory is at times pre-verbal memory i.e. not accompanied by words, and at other times it is verbal memory, i.e. containing words.

In analysis we deal with both types. But people are more tormented by the pre-verbal memory in their efforts to find words and fill gaps. The unknown drives them crazy.

It should be stressed that prohibition and guilt in remembering, knowing and seeking the truth is a common characteristic in these subjects.

Their reality testing is poor; they live between fantasy and reality. Therefore it is not surprising that at the beginning of their analysis, analysands fabricate stories which they believe to be true memories.

Freud (1900) said "*unconscious fantasies become indistinguishable from memories*". In addition to that, a complicated defensive game is played between violence and memory in which violence appears to be in the service of memory; but in fact the opposite happens: memory is in the service and at the mercy of violence. In other words, violence has the upper hand and uses memory to find a way to achieve its ultimate goal which is to be acted out. Analysands are trapped in this defensive game, because escape is prohibited and guilt-ridden due to their psychopathology.

When and if the psychoanalytic process progresses, and as their reality testing improves, they recognize that what they believed to be true memory has been fictional.

My personal experience working with such cases has taught me that the key that opens the door to their memory often lies in previous generations. These previous generations had their own problems of guilt and prohibition in transmitting their knowledge, experience, the history of their lives, etc. Hence they keep secrets and falsify the truth when they recount the family history to their children and grandchildren. For example, a 65-year-old patient of mine who has been suicidal for as long as I've known him, which is 30 years, feels that he is the sum total of all the unspoken secrets in his family. He is now searching secretly in his aged mother's apartment hoping to find the key that will open the door to the secret world.

Several analysts have dealt with this problem, Jacques Hassoun (1994), to name but one, in his book entitled "*Les contrebandiers de la memoire*".

From the developmental point of view violent memory, i.e. affective memory, is "built up in the undifferentiated symbiotic phase in the context of infant-mother interaction under the influence of both gratifying and frustrating experiences" (Kernberg 1982). Kernberg's views (1979, 1982, 1997) are based on those of S. Freud, Jacobson E, M. Mahler, Fairbairn, Klein and Winnicott. Melanie Klein (1945) and her followers, on the other hand, believe that affective memory is developed during the first six months of life. The common element in both views is that the development of affective memory precedes the development of language. Their theoretical differences and controversies are beyond the scope of this paper.

Analysts who have also had experience with children, including Melanie Klein, Hanna Segal, and Clifford Scott, have contributed a great deal to our understanding of the expression, manifestation and communicative aspect of affective behavior in relation to the individual's needs and objects.

In clinical practice, violent memory has the following features. It occurs suddenly and out of the clear blue sky and takes even the subject by surprise, as though it were occurring for the first time. Needless to say it also shocks his or her environment. It is a violent attack from within, which floods the total self. It threatens the homeostasis (omoiostasis) of his own organism, as well, of course, as its relation to the environment.

It forces the subject to act by turning against the self (suicide) or against others (murder) or both, in order to discharge the violence. This is an internal necessity that must be carried out. The trigger point is often unrecognized by the subject. During psychoanalytic sessions it is expressed violently by pre-verbal and verbal means, screaming, yelling, throwing things around and is often accompanied by physical outbursts resembling a child's temper tantrums. The verbal content of violent memory consists of random fragments of memory manifested in words which, as a whole, make no sense. Words, usually derogative, or curses are addressed against their parents and other important persons in their life, and of course against the analyst.

Although the purpose of affective behavior "is to signal to the environment the infant's needs, to initiate communication that marks the beginning of intrapsychic life", (Izard 1978, 1979), these subjects, with their outburst of violence, fail to communicate their needs and wishes either to themselves or to their environment, thus precluding satisfaction of these needs and wishes.

Violent memory is also manifested in dreams and fantasies, especially in well behaved people. It is generally accepted that violent memory is not related to psychiatric diagnostic categories, but to severe traumatic experiences in early life such as the inability of the mothering person to meet the needs of the infant, especially during the subphases of the symbiotic relationship, paternal loss, particularly of the mother, prolonged hospitalization of the mothering person, depression, chronic pain, neglect of the child, exposure to danger, abuse, and finally whatever experience is felt by the child as being traumatic. Kernberg (1982) says "*The effects of the traumatic past reside in the patient's structuralisation of internalized object relations" and he continues by saying that. "This internalized object relation has transformed the primitive affect of rage into a characterologically anchored, chronic disposition of violence which is activated in transference*".

M. Klein says that "*early experiences such as hunger or satisfaction, are experienced and interpreted by the infant in terms of object relations giving them emotional meaning. E.g. a baby in pain may feel itself as being hated*".

To the above we should add the collective national trauma, and in the case of Greece it was the Asia Minor Disaster in 1922, World War II and the Civil War right afterwards. This is very important considering the fact that our analysands are the third generation to be affected one way or another by the national trauma of the previous generation.

The clinical material which follows is from analysands of mine who have displayed manifestations of violent memory. I would like to cite an example of what we have been talking about.

A woman of 40, married with children, who suffered the loss of her mother at the age of five, who was abused and exposed to dangers, has been suicidal and violent throughout her life, and in trouble with the law, has been in treatment for the greater part of her life, going from one therapist to another. She came to one session, just before vacation time and told me the following, weeping and screaming:

"*Yesterday morning, while I was sleeping in the arms of my husband, my husband woke me up and told me to go and open the door because somebody was knocking. I went, gave a person some information, closed the door and then started to yell and scream. I felt there was nothing inside me but violence, and didn't know what to do about it. So I kept screaming and yelling. Then my husband said: 'How can I help you?' and I said: 'Take me in your arms and hold me as tight as you can.' In this way the violence gradually died down and I came back to myself*". She stopped for a minute and then said: "*You know what I think all this screaming meant?*" It said: "*Look after me. Do something for me*". This was how she interpreted her non verbal violent memory.

The trigger point, from what we can understand, was the interruption of a symbiotic moment in her life - sleeping in her husband's arms. The reference to the analyst is evident. It was just before the summer vacation, which for her meant the disaster of separation from her analyst.

She went on: "*My life now is very good, but it's like I don't fit in here. I have a strong urge to go back to the old family atmosphere where violence was bread and butter. Memories of violence are inside me but the words are missing. I feel some action should be taken. Before I can go on in life I must either commit a murder or kill myself*".

She is a good-looking woman, successful in her profession, sociable, and manages to keep her home and her family going.

The clinical material which follows is from analysands of mine following cancellation of an appointment on the previous day.

I made the cancellations myself by leaving messages on their answering machine without mentioning the reasons for the cancellation. However from what emerged in the next session, it became evident that the tone of my voice had betrayed that some serious life event had occurred.

A 34-year-old woman brought the following dream. "I *was biting my mother ferociously and telling her that I'd go to my grandmother and never see her again*". Her grandmother, who had brought her up, had died recently. This dream occurred on the first night the analysand had slept all alone in her new apartment.

Her associations to the dream were: "*I was all alone - nobody called. My mother has not called me over the past few days. I' m sure that my mother doesn't want me to have a family, she wants to keep me like a beggar, bringing me food in little plastic containers. You, too, make me feel incapable of going on and progressing. I keep many secrets from you. The obsessive image of cutting my own throat keeps coming to me. When I am working, I feel that someone is coming after me with a gun. There is a lid that keeps all this from coming out. It all comes back to me when I'm left alone. You keep secrets too. You kept secret the reason why you cancelled our appointment. But someone told me what happened to you...*"

Another analysand, a 30-year-old woman, came to her session with the following dream: "*I was back home. My parents were there. I climbed up to get something off a high shelf and when I tried to get down, something pushed me and I fell to the floor. In the dream I thought that my parents would think that I had tried to kill myself*".

Her associations to the dream: "*I keep thinking about Miss B. who committed suicide when her therapist cancelled her appointment. My parents have not called me for the past five days. We are like strangers*".

A 32-year-old women came to her session following the cancellation of our appointment and said:

"*The cancellation of the appointment has something to do with death. I was an unwanted child, I feel like a wounded animal. Maybe I' m fond of you maybe not. I dreamed that you were a vampire who drinks my blood. In our sessions you are trying to learn my secret, to drink my blood. For me to become creative, I must first commit a murder, I must kill those who have made me end up the way I am*".

It is obvious that the cases presented above cannot face separation due to the cancellation of an appointment or due to vacations. This separation caused regression resulting in dreams containing violence against themselves or others. The concretization of their dreams is also a manifestation of their regression.

Their parents and grandparents suffer from some kind of national trauma. In their families, violent quarrels are frequent, as are deaths, suicides, and alcoholism. In other words the analysands live in an atmosphere of some kind of violence in the narrow or broader sense of the word. All of them have been in psychotherapy for a good part of their lives, going from one therapist to another. It is possible that they have been looking for someone who can bear the intensity of their feelings and foster their symbiotic needs.

We have said that psychoanalysis defends life, but before going on to discuss this, we should point out the feature that characterizes the people whose lives we are trying to defend. My clinical observations (in analyzing this particular group of people) coincide with those put forward by other analysts such as Kernberg, Segal, Klein, Rosenfelt, Claude Balier 1998.

All these subjects have the fear and dread of being abandoned, they wish to be in their mother's arms, a wish forbidden and therefore disguised. Often they live between dreams and reality. They are confused about their personal history. They feel that their ancestors contributed to their confused mental state either by remaining silent or by transmitting falsified experience to them, as described above. However they prefer to live in this confusion rather than to ask questions of their parents or grandparents. The analysands feel that they have been left out of their ancestors' secrets and have no right to disrupt this spurious balance. They accept whatever they are told even though they may doubt its truth.

Freud (1920) saw that "the basic psychic conflict is that between the life and death instinct". Acting in and acting out are used to discharge their violent projective identification, to get rid of psychic content, and to minimalise internal terror and violence. Suicide is the ultimate relief from the conflictual psychic state. Outbursts of violence due to non-verbal memory - histoire sans paroles - are frequent in sessions.

The analysands are fixated on their mother or mother substitute. They try to create symbiotic relationships in which interruption provokes terror and violence. In analysis they are reluctant to pass on their own or their family's violent thoughts and history. They are afraid that the analyst will be frightened and unable to contain them.

In analysis they try to develop a symbiotic type of relationship which seems to be confined to their fantasy. They say: "*Only when I come here do I feel alive, I have wishes and plans; when I leave, everything is over*".

It is questionable whether their way of working through is genuine or remains on the level of fantasy. Others do not really care about working through. But they do care about maintaining the symbiotic relationship with the analyst on their own terms.

Dreams are another way of acting in and acting out, as Freud said. Kleinians have the same views. The dreams of the analysands presented above are mainly used by the dreamers to discharge their affects and to evacuate their mental contents (Bion 1958). They function as symbolic equations rather than as symbolic communication. (Segal 1978) The aim of evacuating into the object-analyst is twofold. One is to split off and get rid of psychic contents and the second is to affect the analyst. In psychoanalytic sessions there is a re-enactment of the dream content. These analysands often bring dreams that are uncontainable.

Segal (1991) reminds us that there are dreams uncontainable in the session, such as those in which there is a crudity in symbolization. Analysands experience the dream as a concrete event, blurring the boundaries between internal and external objects, features that we meet in the dreams of the case presented above.

The envy of the analyst is often present. The containing function of the analyst is often attacked. In this case the danger is that the transference-countertransference relationship may become mutually destructive or end up in a folie a deux. And thus, equipped with our understanding of these analysands' psychopathology, we are called upon to defend their lives.

This is easy to say and difficult to do. However my experience finds me in agreement with Kernberg (1997) as well as with Hanna Segal (1991), who says: "*First and above all, the Analyst has to provide a container which restores the mental space and helps to restore the symbolic function and enable them to face the separation of a holiday*" or of the cancellation of an appointment without causing them such a regression. Working through takes place in this atmosphere, with caution, avoiding premature comments or interpretations. Regarding the interpretations of their dreams, one must first interpret the effect it is supposed to have on the analyst and only gradually can one then address the content of the dreams (Segal, Kernberg, Greenberg).

Eventually the analysand's memory is restored, but never completely. They must be helped to come to terms with and accept the fact that the truth about their lives cannot be fully grasped and that they must go on living, even though the question "*why did I end up this way?*" has been only partially understood.

As a result, their capacity to tolerate the unknown improves; acting out subsides and of course the risk of a final act fades.

Conclusions

The foregoing supports the view that violent memory is a warning of imminent suicide or murder, that it is related to severe traumatic experience in early life and to the separation individuation phase of development.

Our experience indicates that psychoanalysis can defend the life of individuals who are tormented by violent memories, and thus prevent suicidal acts, providing that both analyst and analysand vote for life (are in favor of life). If one of them is against life, then the final outcome is doubtful.

From the foregoing we can conclude that the work of the psychoanalyst is supported if the interplay between the "contained and the container" is benign, and if the analyst can accept his own limitations, those of his analysand and those of psychoanalysis when applied to such cases.

2. Violence in cases of adults: 4 cases

Case 1. Testimony Year 2005

In this paper, we shall be hearing the testimony of a 50-year-old hero who, along the way, became the guilty party. The content of this testimony, especially his "fever of murder" towards his wife, appeared for the first time in 2005, despite the fact that he had been in analysis with the writer for the past thirty years, with brief interruptions, the longest of which was his eight years of marriage.

He returned to analysis in the year 2005. What sparked the events in the analysand's inner world that unfolded in this testimony, and in particular what he calls the "fever of murder", was the fact that his wife left him.

One wonders what caused such a violent reaction. Did someone desert him in the past, and if so who? Had he deserted someone? Or both? What he said previously covers just one aspect, that desertion is a familiar theme to him, because in his childhood and adolescence he was repeatedly deserted by both his parents for periods of varying duration. They would always return to the family, where they remain to this day. The other aspect however, is unknown, i.e. whether he has deserted other people and if so, who? We do know that eight years ago, the analysand got married and discontinued his analysis without notification. This, according to his own laws, constituted desertion of the psychoanalyst.

His wife initially adored him as a hero because he had rescued her from a disturbed, problematic family environment, married her, protected her, taken care of her in every way and helped her to overcome her personal shortcomings, mental and practical. However, during the course of their married life, she gradually became cruel and abusive; she humiliated him, put him down, was unfaithful to him, blamed him for everything, destroyed him financially and slowly changed his secure status of hero to that of the guilty party, eventually punishing him with the "ultimate penalty" of desertion, when she left him to seek happiness with another man. The analysand had to accept the unavoidable and in 2005 returned to analysis, which he continues.

The testimony of the analysand consists of a number of sessions and is presented in its actual succession as faithfully as possible.

Year 2005

First Session

The moment the analysand entered the analyst's office, he announced: "*I'm ruined, I've had a breakdown, I can't work, I have no money and how will I be able to pay?*" (meaning the analyst). He howled and cried, sobbing inconsolably. He had neglected his appearance; he was unshaven and his hair was uncombed - all unusual for him. He declared: "*There is a fever inside me, because I came in contact with the desire to kill. I wasn't frightened - this is the dark side of myself that I have always hidden and shown another - nice, kind, amenable, performing services for my wife and everybody [weeping, mixed with shouts and anger] - I wanted to cut off her head and have some peace - she uprooted me and threw me away like an uprooted child. The guilt exists before the crime.*"

I wondered what guilt and what crime he was implying. "*I read Dostoyevski's Brothers Karamazov and calmed down. Dimitri killed his wretched father for a woman. The monk kisses the feet of the miserable Old Man Karamazov because he recognises how much he has suffered. The greatest works are on the theme of patricide. Solomos was an illegitimate child. His father never acknowledged him - there were court cases. Solomos never wrote a complete work. Fragments of diamonds. I want to bring what I am feeling out into the open - not to kill in reality. I had a fight with my superior. I answered him as was proper - I was right. When the fever of murder comes upon me, I keep your voice in my mind and that calms me and protects me from killing someone.*"

Second session

"*I got up this morning - sadness and guilt, a familiar feeling from way back.*"

I wondered what had happened to him in the past to cause sadness and guilt. It is not known to me, and I do not comment.

"I feel that I am unworthy, I am nothing, it takes me a very long time to feel better. I talk to myself and tell myself - Man, you're stupid, pull yourself together." He burst into tears.

"Sadness and guilt because I didn't tell my father the truth. I used to cover for my mother who was a whore. Everything they put in my mind was like a transplant encapsulated. My father's relatives said it was my fault my mum became a whore."

I accept what he tells me but I believe that there are deeper reasons which, for the moment, are not known to me and are associated with the great sorrow and guilt the analysand feels. I make no comment.

It should be noted that, from the time the analysand was a child, his mother used him as an alibi and for this reason would take him with her to meetings with various men. He said he was a silent eyewitness to sexual contacts without being able to object.

"You know, the only genuine feeling I have is loneliness - as a child, especially on Sundays. I had no home, I had no place to go. I would wander the streets. I used to go to a coffee shop that adults frequented, they liked me, they accepted me."

Third session

"Last night I wet my bed. My wife accuses me of being to blame for everything, even for the cancer she came down with."

From his mobile phone, he read me some of her written messages that confirmed what he was saying.

"I felt like a murderer. The fever of murder rose up in me to kill her, to kill. I have inside me a can with punishments that I deal out ... for every good thing that happens to me. I had a dream. I was at my mother's house - she is in bed waiting for a man. There is a knock at the door. I open it. Two men arrive to make love to my mother. I do nothing..."

"You know at church, after the service and while everybody is

still inside, the sinner tells his sins in silence (after the priest reads a prayer)."

Fourth session

"*I went to my mother's house, I asked about her and about my father, I wanted to learn more. My mother told me that my father had committed a murder when he was young. Before he got married he killed a friend of his for a lark - he was drunk and was playing with the victim who begged him on his knees not to kill him but finally he killed him. The whores he hung around with hid him, and he was acquitted by the court. That was when he met my mother. After that my father became an alcoholic. That was the only time I ate a meal at my mother's house without throwing up (so far every time I ate at my mother's house I would throw up). I invited my mother to come and stay at my house for a few days*"

The analyst reflected, without making any comment to the analysand, on the reconciliation of mother and son. They are no longer separated by the secret (father-murderer). The murder had already taken place, so it was not necessary for him to commit murder. Later we learned that other murders had taken place in his close family environment.

Thus the inner world of the analysand was disclosed. Six months after beginning this period of analysis (2005), he stated that he had committed the offence of the centuries when he was 13 years old, when he decided to desert his family to save himself. He evolved into a presentable, charismatic young man, who excelled in his high school and university studies, which meant that to his sin of abandoning his family was added the sin of *hubris,* which in Greek means the gross offence of standing out. "*I shot up much higher than my own orbit,*" he said, i.e. he rose above the level of his family, thereby damaging its honour. It should be pointed out that he always managed to ensure moral and material backing and support from important officials, carefully suppressing his "*sins*". For 30 years, he maintained this same stance with his analyst, who had felt that he was hiding many things but did not know what.

Here ends the testimony of the 50-year-old analysand given in 2005 and consisting of a number of sessions as we saw above.

In this paper, the relationship between the couple will not be discussed, nor the personality of his wife, nor the content of protagonist's previous analysis from the beginning to 2005. Only the information deemed necessary for the understanding of this material will be presented as an exception to this rule.

Note: his father died some years ago of a serious physical illness. Up to the end, the analysand looked after him with care and love. "*I pampered him,*" he says.

Dynamics

If one were attempting to describe in a few words the dynamics of the analysand's personality, one would say that he is a man of good appearance, charming, highly intelligent and educated; at the same time he is regarded as a gross insult *(hubris)* to his family, which is of a limited financial, social and educational level, and looked down on by the community they live in because the family events are known. In addition, he is looked down on by his environment, because his family events are known to the small community he lives in.

Initially, the child defends first one parent and then the other without effect; he cannot bring balance to the family. The quarrels between his parents were daily and violent. The intervention of the police was a not infrequent occurrence. As a result, he was left alone, as he said; he did not know where to go, he suffered, and felt stifled by the "*seething cauldron inside me*", full of contradictions, conflicts, guilt and desires. His greatest desire was to get away from his family.

At the same time his family kept pressuring him and assigning him the role of hero, i.e. to save his family and deliver it from its dead-end life.

He seized the opportunity and shouldered the role of hero, but only to save himself. He abandoned his family and escaped from the stifling environment, leaving behind the poor, degraded family with no prospects. He was 13 years old. He left home - a provincial city -

and came to the capital of Athens where he evolved into a bright star from all viewpoints, in terms of character and ethics, and in terms of performance in high school and university studies. He was an excellent student, enjoyed the esteem of his university professors, of people in his employment environment and in his social life.

Sadness and above all anger dominate his psychological state. "*Guilt precedes the crime,*" he stated.

That is, along the way our hero became the guilty party, selecting the type of guilt, that is the guilt of the hero - and hubris. He arrived at a point where he was unable to handle the role of hero and its implications, especially his guilt, and suffered a breakdown. He was unable to write his final examinations in order to graduate from university. That was the reason he came into analysis 30 years ago; it helped him to acquire his degree and indeed with high marks.

The "offence" is dual - first the desertion of his paternal family, and second the *hubris.*

In 2005, the protagonist broke down once again, but the conditions were reversed. This time, the dual "offence" was committed by his wife: desertion by her and *hubris* to save herself and to live in happiness with a "brighter" star. That was when the analysand sought help once again and returned to analysis.

Along the way, the hero had succeeded in becoming the guilty party and in reversing the conditions, thus leading his wife to the role of "hero", i.e. hubris. Throughout his life, the analysand played the role of hero at every opportunity that arose, but in the process, he became the guilty party, with a fitting punishment. And this was what gave him balance. His marriage was an opportunity of this kind, as he selected a woman who would play his psychological game. But this time, i.e. in 2005, he found the punishment imposed on him by his wife, i.e. desertion, disproportionately great.

It was like the moment when his personal destiny fused with the destiny of circumstances and created an explosion - the fever of murder towards his wife. According to this reasoning, it was he who triggered the fever of murder in his family when he deserted them to save only himself.

The analysand tried to deceive both himself and the analyst by linking the "fever of murder" solely with his wife's desertion, suppressing his own dual offence, i.e. deserting his family - "a punishable act, unforgivable, deplorable" and *hubris.*

This is how the writer understands the dynamics of the analysand's personality, a viewpoint that has been confirmed in his on-going analysis and documented by transference.

At this point in the analysis, ten months after the testimony of his "fever of murder", the way in which he has chosen to handle his own guilt is to deal with the guilt of his parents and grandparents. This defensive manoeuvre has been noted, as has his strong tendency to make new self-destructive moves.

In my view, we are witnesses to the above processes, but also to his genuine desire to limit the tragic nature of his personality.

Transference - Countertransference

Year 2005

Even though the presence of transference-countertransference is obvious from the above, nevertheless it is judged necessary to comment on it separately.

Transference appeared in the first session of this analytic period; it was regressive and continues to be so. It brings to light the analysand's deeper self, his inner world. He declared "*I am ruined ... I have no money to pay you*" (the analyst).

I thought he was looking for trouble, provoking me, testing me. Whatever I did, the game was his: if I did not agree to his remaining in analysis without paying a fee, he would have succeeded in getting what he wanted, i.e. desertion by me. And if I had agreed, he would also have succeeded in getting what he wanted, i.e. to be accepted on his own terms, and to transform me from "hero" to "guilty party".

I decided on the second course - without making any comment. I applied the technique of silent containment and silent interpretation, with the dynamic they embody. This meant that I accepted his terms as well as the technique proposed by him, the silent containment which corresponds to what he himself declared: "The sinner in the church in front of the entire congregation confesses his sins in silence". In other words, the analysand (sinner) begs the psychoanalyst to respect his singularity and his breakdown, and to help him deal with his inner conflicts, above all the "fever of murder", without comment. In silence.

The analysand said. "*When the fever of murder comes upon me, your voice is always inside me calming me and I stop*", which means that the fever is not transformed into action - he idealises his analyst and attributes to her omnipotent capabilities. His intention of splitting the object is perceived, as are his threats; he warns me and threatens to lie in wait for me if I dare to accuse him or desert him; if I provoke the "fever of murder", I will have the same fate as his wife.

I decided that the technique to follow was what seemed appropriate at the given moment, i.e. silent containment which contains not only his verbal testimony but also his emotional outbursts, rage, threats, weeping, shouts, etc. Then he said that if I rejected him he would feel the same way as when his wife rejected him: "*She threw me out like an uprooted child*".

Continuing, he proposed the technique that he would like the psychoanalyst to follow. "*The monk kisses the feet of the father Karamazov because he recognises how much he has suffered.*"

The analysand and his demand shed further light on his personality. He identified himself with the poet Dionysios Solomos. He informed his analyst that "*this illegitimate child [Solomos], son of the Count and his mother, the servant*" (mother - whore), created "*fragmentary diamonds*", "*but not a complete work*". Our analysand informed us that he has suffered the same fate as Solomos - that he, too, creates "*fragmentary diamonds*" with his excellent studies but fragmentary jobs. His human relations, too, are fragmentary. He identifies himself with his mother (whore) and the mother of Solomos (servant). He declares that his own behaviour is usually that of the paid whore: he writes dissertations, articles, etc, for minimal fees, allowing his clients to underestimate him and humiliate him, and from a "hero" to change him into the "guilty party".

"*Continuing to shed light on his personality, he never loved me, he never recognised me, he never satisfied my demands - the image I have of him is blurred*" meaning his father.

Which means that he suffered deprivations and psychic battering from both his parents during childhood and adolescence. We realise that what has priority at this moment for him is to secure the sympathy and acceptance of his analyst, rather than to understand his own inner world.

Regarding countertransference, there is a danger that the psychoanalyst might fall into the traps set by the analysand and possibly become the object of his "fever of murder", which could be fatal for both the interested parties, psychoanalyst and analysand. The psychoanalytic process continues and the analysand, despite all, is highly motivated to be relieved of his psychic pain and to live a more optimistic life.

In conclusion, it was in the year 2005 that the personal destiny of our hero was fused with the destiny of circumstances and especially that of his wife, and caused the outbreak of the "fever of murder", which in an extremely painful way gave him the opportunity to come in contact with some unknown parts of his unconscious and then to work through them.

On the other hand, it not until 2005, i.e. after 30 years of analysis, that the analyst witnessed the analysand's psychotic core, the fever of murder.

Within the context of transference, the analyst became the target of the "fever of murder" in a complex ambivalent manner. The analysand sought to transform the "hero" - the analyst - into the "guilty party", by leading her to a compulsory "silence" and to possible desertion by not being at all reliable in his financial obligations, and by his aggressive behaviour and his threats against her.

Case 2. Between violence and inertness

A crying baby

The culmination of the violence within which a 32-year-old analysand lived was the Stabbing, i.e. attempted murder with a knife that occurred in her father's family, with which she had close links. Her violent father solves all his differences by taking the law into his own hands.

The culmination of the Inertness within which the analysand lived was her mother.

The culmination of her own identifications was identification with stabbing as an autonomous action and a value in itself, and identification with the Stabber. The offender was led to this act because he was unjustly treated. With the stabbing, he was attempting to punish the person who had been unjust to him, i.e. his mother. Instead, he found himself being punished by the courts for taking the law into his own hands. This means that the analysand identifies with the Offender and takes on his dynamic, i.e. she is constantly prepared to pull out a knife when she feels she is not being treated fairly. For the time being, it is worth noting that the lover with whom she had the longest relationship has the same name and surname as the stabber (no relation). The analysand also identifies with the Inert Mother. This identification becomes obvious when she deals with frustration and when she is threatened.

Her inert mother "*never goes out of the house and lives in semi-voluntary retirement, without feeling, speaking in dull platitudes, with emaciated hands that you hope will never touch you, who never hugged me, who has never convinced me that she loves me, never taught me anything, and was completely submissive to the violent but emotional father. Whenever he was having a violent crisis, my father would shout at her: 'Get out of my sight because I'll kill you.' And she - my mother - would leave.*"

The analysand also witnessed her father's physical and verbal violence against other people, e.g. employees etc. With her, however he confined himself to verbal violence. "*Ever since I was a child, whenever my father raised his voice, my legs would turn to jelly and*

I didn't dare talk back to him or fight with him - and still don't. I am afraid of his anger."

Violence dominates her personality and is the main theme in her analysis "*Who will stab whom, who will stab first?*"

The expressions she uses to describe her relations with friends, colleagues etc. are the following: "*He took the ball away from me - I had to do something*", "*he threw down the gauntlet, I picked it up - what else could I do?*" etc. She says: "*I feel like I am standing in two boats trying to bring my legs together - two boats two parents. I am afraid of my inertness (mother) - it's like one leg stays behind and won't let me go forward and create - like I am weighed down and can't move, I do different things but I can't move ahead - I'm like my father - I don't create - he does lots of things too, girlfriends, work, but he can't get ahead - if he could, he would have separated, he would have married again, at work he would have done very well, he has capabilities.*"

The dead end and lack of creativity in which she lives can be seen in the following repeated dream: "*I was in a house with rooms without doors - to go from one room to another you had to go through windows instead of doors. For me, the dream means that the transition is difficult - to take examinations to finish the Master's, to stay home for a while without working, without money. I'll have to find a job, and find money. Black May came and I see you once every two weeks or not at all. I've got no money.*"

"*You know that I've got a knife, I don't know where I'll stick it, but I'm afraid that I'll go over the edge and lose control. One of my feet standing in inertness and the other in stabbing. I'm afraid I'll be torn in two I'll go over the edge. I can't be in the same place with either my father or with my boyfriend. I can't live with anyone, I'm afraid of the violence coming out - I can't bridge anything different. There are some things in them (father and boyfriend) that I don't appreciate. I have invited Kostas to go with me to the Conference. We'll be together for 5 days. What will happen? I'm afraid of the stabbing.*" When she came back from the conference, she said: "*Kostas robbed me of the conference. I didn't attend at all, I was obliged to keep him company*". At the end of the trip, "*I asked him what he felt about me - Nothing he said, we just have a good time together. So we broke up, we each went our own way, and since then I haven't heard a word from him, not even a phone call.*"

In this case the analysand, unable to stand the anxiety over what would happen between them, provoked the split - she pulled out her knife.

"*I met a migrant doctor. We met, nothing happened, I can't stand the internal pressure. I want to sleep with him soon to stop the threat of whether he will accept or reject me, so I can relax. The body never tells lies. I'll sleep with Yannis to let myself go. Otherwise I won't be able to stand it, I need to know - Yes or no. I can't work, I can't do anything. That's why I've slept with so many men. I want sex right away. When I was little I used to wonder whether my father was coming home that night or not. I lived in anxiety.*"

The analysand moves between inertness and violence. When she is neither inert nor violent she is a baby crying and asking for help so that she can escape from the bipole of inertness and violence, to grow out of it and evolve into an autonomous, and above all creative, person. This was why she came into analysis. The analysand is anxious and has to fight not to give in to her tendency to be inert and to become a "block of wood" like her mother. It is even more difficult for her to deal with and control the strong attraction she feels drawing her to violence (her father and his family).

Anxiety floods her. She continues: "*I am afraid that I am transparent and that other people can see my weaknesses. I am afraid of inertness. I am afraid of the identifications I make - I identify with my father's girlfriends, with deviations, with transvestites, with homosexuals. With violent people. I dreamed that you told me I needed a guardian.*"

The ways in which she handles the primeval violence that is constantly pressuring her is through her identifications, stabbing, the violent men, etc. By projecting it, by transferring it and giving it form wherever she finds it, by putting it into practice like the sexual act and "venting her anger" as she says, by rehashing it in her sessions in the hope of understanding it better. All these efforts ultimately aim to prevent the final act - stabbing on the symbolic or non-symbolic level. From the above it can be concluded that she has not succeeded in fully escaping from the storm of her inner world. This is why she lived alone for a while, but she didn't like it, and is obsessed with finding a companion. She complains: "*On the weekend, my computer and I feel very lonely. I dreamed that we, you and I, are in a playground with horizontal bars doing acrobatics - and you drop dead. I cry, and then, at your house, you open a chest of drawers where the drawers are in perfect order; you look through them to find a present for me of gold bracelets - but they're handcuffs. The dream made an impression on me, because it means you have to give me everything in perfect order,*" and she weeps constantly (feeling that I have treated her unjustly).

Thus flowed the analysand's inner life. At the same time, however, she was able to finish her Master's degree and then took examinations for a very good job in the public service. Here she was weighing two solutions: one of becoming a civil servant which, for her, meant inert security, but also obedience to the Great Powers in following her mother's path; the other of daring to choose a freelance profession and become an independent and creative person. She decided on the latter.

For the first time, she took an initiative and called her parents to meet all together (violence and inertness). She discussed with them her desire to be independent. Her parents agreed and stated that they would help her in every way - which they did. She came and told me about the meeting with her parents and her decision to take up freelance work and said: "*I feel that I have come of age now. I don't believe that my parents are together - and my father was so nice.*" "*We have already started the preparations. I can hardly believe it. I am happy. We have achieved many things together.*" In this last phrase she meant that she, with the collaboration of the analyst, has succeeded in achieving many things on the university, professional and personal level.

She continued saying that she wanted to break off with her current boyfriend who has the same first and last name as "the Stabber" (although they are totally unrelated). "*I'll do it slowly, but surely.*" In these words she is indirectly asking the analyst to give her plenty of time to make this break.

That is, the analysand wants to de-identify herself - she feels she no longer needs to use violence to achieve her goals - stabbing as a way of life, as a way of having a relationship.

Dynamics

From the above it is clear that the analysand was living under extremely conflicting and contradictory conditions that overcame her. It was natural that she expended an enormous amount of p-sychic energy in order to secure her own psychic survival, since the demands were disproportionately great for her age. As a result, there was only a slim chance that she would develop and evolve normally and evenly.

She was, however, lucky in that her father is an ambitious man who supported her in her studies in every way, emotionally and materially. He allowed her to surpass him in terms of education and professional career and on the social level.

She herself is an intelligent person seized the opportunity and succeeded in her high school, university and post-graduate studies, learned foreign languages, etc.

We are aware that her university studies and professional career constitute her most important defence mechanism that enables her to deal with her chaotic inner storm.

It should be stressed that the unconscious core that she was very carefully concealing is the crying baby - the hopeless, impotent, inert baby asking for help. She delivered the above state in her fourth year of analysis, when she was unable to cope with her professional career. This means that the violence defended the crying baby, i.e. violence was a cover for the crying baby, because violence made her feel strong.

Transference - countertransference

I will not say more about her family situation, or any other aspects of her analysis, nor will I analyse the material that has already been presented. This I will leave to the reader.

I will, however, comment on the transference-countertransference axis in this case.

It is judged necessary to describe the atmosphere in which the transference-countertransference unfolded.

The analysand is now 32 years old and going through her fourth year of analysis. She is presentable, carefully dressed and likeable, but overweight.

The moment she walks in, she fills the session room with a mixture of unprocessed, undifferentiated anxiety and a sense of violence which she exudes permanently, sometimes with a different level of intensity, like a storm that is about to break.

This is the canvas (like background music) on which the hectic material, her discourse, is painted.

We are not unaware of the effort she makes to conceal her tension and to remain polite and formal. This observation constitutes the positive signal of transference to the analyst. Thus, the primal demand to which the analyst is called upon to respond is to contain the storm of her emotions - which as a technique the writer finds feasible but not easy. For greater clarity it should be pointed out that in this particular case, the container communicates in a non-verbal manner what she would have said in words i.e. acceptance or non-acceptance, and the analysand understands it. As an example, I mention that when she stated that a friend was going abroad for further training and asked her to go with him - she said - "*I refused because I thought that Mrs Alexandri would not permit it.*" To silently contain here constituted an affirmation of the technique that I have chosen.

She is always formal, polite and tries to be liked and accepted by her analyst. But when she cannot handle her violent feelings towards the analyst, and cannot conceal or control them, she cancels her session, and has the tendency to run away from the analytic process. For example she states sometimes that a friend of hers who is leaving for further studies abroad for a year or two asked her to go with him. Then she said: "*I thought that Mrs Alexandri would not permit it.*" It is obvious that she projects her own prohibition onto the analyst because she realises that it would be self-destructive for her to interrupt her studies and leave the country.

At the same time she was, of course, testing me as to whether I want her to stay as an analysand and as a person, or whether I would rather she left. I should say that periodically I have doubts as to whether the analysand will remain in analysis i.e. whether she has a good enough object, as Klein would have said.

The violence and punishment meted out to the analyst is presented in the dream in which she is dead and puts handcuffs instead of bracelets on the analysand. In the end she asked me to help her to sort out the storm of her inner world and her internal objects.

Violence is projected in the form of punishments - I tell her that she needs a guardian.

As for the analyst, it has often been difficult to tolerate and contain the analysand's high anxiety level and underlying despair.

Case 3. The Glass Bowl

The clinical material presented here was generated in my office in 2004 during one session. The 40-year-old analysand delivered his inner world to me - his analyst - in the eighth year of his analysis. All along it was obvious to me that he was not 100% with me and that part of him was excluded. This was the main reason that he entered analysis. He wanted to "live his daily life as a whole person" as he put it.

He was having tremendous difficulties with his relationships. What triggered the content of this session was the analysand's frustration with a friendship, which he was unable to handle emotionally.

He entered my office, sat down opposite me and said: "*I sit with a glass bowl in front of me, cross-legged like the seer who tells fortunes. I am holding a pair of tweezers with which I remove Yannis, who is inside the glass bowl, so that I can play with him. I play with him and then I leave him aside and he goes back into the bowl.*"

"*The glass bowl is life or the daily routine in which people live, I sit outside this, because I am at risk owing to my special traits. I control them all, some are permanently in the bowl, others go in and out like Kostas, and my Mum. I am God. It sounds crazy, I imagine Yannis [a friend of his] inside the bowl lying on his back and not knowing what to do.*"

At the next session he said that when he left my office (after delivering his psychic core), he felt relieved because finally he related to his analyst at a total person. He comments on the previous session. "*I took a sudden, unexpected plunge into my own thoughts which I had never before experienced. I see myself as a solitary, tall man, presentable, healthy and strong who sits in front of his glass bowl in a quiet room. Inside the bowl, I can see only the figure of Yannis, lying on his back as though he had assumed the shape of the bowl. He is also the only one of my friends whom I can see clearly in the bowl.*"

The empty room in which he lives is for him a point of departure. "The glass bowl is my only road to escape, I dip briefly into the lives of my friends. In my friend Pavlos's life, I share some time with him from my own life. At the same time, I go like a transit route, for meetings with other friends, and I'm almost never anywhere as a whole person. A part of me is with them, while another is back in my room in front of the glass bowl, waiting to return from short trips up and down. Whatever small outings I make from the room, which can be for short or long periods, there seems to be some basic trace that remains there (in the room), while its reflection is cast far away, as though linked together with springs. However much these springs are stretched, they will function in such a way as to bring my more social self back to isolation (room). The exception in this discontinuous and fragmentary world was my acquaintanceship with Peter in which the following thing happened. He is very inconsistent, unstable and sometimes unpredictable, but in some magic way I managed with his presence to leave my room altogether, to travel as a whole person outside my room, to be present as a total person with him. [Peter is the same age and has the same profession].

"I had a strong desire to learn as much as I could about him, to have him guide me through his childhood and wherever he had his most significant experiences."

"Rarely have I lived a story of this kind, but it was very tiring. Fortunately it is no more. Because he deserted me."

"If I want to come back to the glass bowl I can see nothing but Yannis. I can see myself, in the secure and total isolation of my room. The man, myself, is healthy, robust, and expects to live long, although he has grown quite a lot older; but he hopes. I would like to live my daily life as a total person."

"For the time being, I am present-absent-everywhere even when I am sitting in front of the sea, which for me is reality."

This words were spoken in one session alone, after his friend Peter went away, and ultimately, deserted him.

This was the first time the analyst found him so upset and disturbed. His mother, when she saw him so upset, advised him to take some medication to help him handle his inner disturbance, which he did.

From what we know, his family failed to fulfil his emotional needs. In addition, he was sent to stay with his grandmother for long periods. The old woman was unable to look after the young boy. He remembers himself feeling that he was different from other children of his age. He did not know what to do with his life and gradually isolated himself.

He was always a good student and very good at university. In addition he is successful in his profession, with a high capacity for work and, of course, he is a very intelligent person.

It is clear from the above that the analysand has warned us what will happen to him if the analyst deserts him: he will go insane.

It is worth noting that he is very formal, polite and tries very hard to be cooperative. He tries to control the sessions by preparing the subjects he wants to talk about. Quite frequently he asks the analyst for advice, mainly about problems in his social life. Recently there have been moments when he relates to the analyst as a total person. He never misses sessions, because it is very important for him to see the analyst. I am inclined to think that I am the reference point regarding his life.

To gain insight or to work through his difficulties is for him secondary. However, he continues his analysis and appears to be more relaxed.

Case 4. Death Order

The history of the "death order" - the settlement of which its 45-year old recipient, the analysand, constantly suppresses, postpones, transfers and tries to annul - will be recounted here. Throughout his life the analysand has tried desperately to deflect this "order" from its target - his own death - and to re-target it to other persons, usually women, who have treated him unjustly and subjected him to financial "blood-letting". He stated:

"*For as long as I can remember, the people in my family find ways to extract money from me.*" He is referring in particular to his mother, his wife and his sisters. For him, this was blood-letting. The "death order" was issued by his parents: his mother had the idea of draining him financially down to his last penny, and his father was drawn in and eventually agreed. Chronologically, the issuing of the "death order" coincided with the time the analysand started working, then a boy of 7-8 years old.

He worked hard and was well paid. When his parents saw what a good and reliable worker he was, they used a label to describe him, saying: "*He'll always manage*". They themselves, on the contrary, were unable to manage, either to have a steady job or to run their household: they were constantly in debt. It seems to the author that the possible motivation for the parents' issuing the "death order" for their son was narcissistic jealousy, combined with the fear that the boy would run away from home, causing them to lose their precious source of money. His punishment was the "death order".

The analysand, as we shall see, did manage, in his parents' terms. For himself, however, managing meant being able to escape, to be relieved of the "death order" that threatened his life. He declared: "*I will not be able to manage; I am afraid that I will not be able to manage.*"

His parents regarded his sisters as useless, by saying: "*They're worth nothing*", and forced them to work in factories. In this way they escaped the death order, but not the order to labour and of course to hand over their earnings to their parents. The analysand would take any job he could find, mainly low-paying heavy work disproportionate to his age. His mother would lie in wait for him and grab his money as soon as he was paid, leaving him just a few pennies. The analysand experienced this action on the part of his mother as "blood-letting". He remembers that when he was 12 years old he gave his mother a sharp push and knocked her over when she went to snatch his hard-earned wages. His action frightened him very much.

Both his parents worked. His father drank any money he made, and became involved in fights after which he would wind up in police custody. The father's penalty was always a fine. The boy would manage to get his father out of prison by collecting the amount of money required, by asking acquaintances and even strangers to contribute anything they could. His mother worked occasionally as a cleaning woman.

Poverty, bad management and violence were the main features of his family life. The lives of the analysand's grandparents were much the same on both the mother's and father's side of the family. It is clear that money was the reason for violent family exchanges. One wonders what had happened to the love between the members of this family. This question will be answered later.

This was how our protagonist grew up. He remembers that in his childhood he was very much alone, without friends, wandering around among the people in the small community in which he lived. This wandering was for him *pas d'enseignement,* pas de douleur (C.P. Baudelaire, 1857).

In elementary school, he barely managed to pass from one grade to the next. His teachers regarded him as a marginal character and a potential delinquent.

The turning point in his life was the sympathy and interest shown to him by one of his teachers, as a result of which, he excelled in his subsequent studies at high school and university.

The analysand's Achilles' heel, which always activated his anger, was injustice, especially financial injustice, when family members, his mother, sisters, and wife would all try to extract money from him. The analysand experienced this behaviour on the part of his family as endless blood-letting. He himself succumbed to the "death order" i.e. this blood-letting, all his life; he gave in to the constant financial demands of his mother, his sisters and his wife. In addition, he borrowed to pay their bills, and signed as guarantor for their loans, which he would eventually have to pay off. He was weak and unable to resist. He was afraid that if things continued in the same way, he would die of the blood-letting. He was inundated with rage and could see no way out, other than by identifying with his parents; in other words, he became the issuer, instead of the recipient, of this death order. This defensive manoeuvre reduced his anxiety and made him feel that he might be able to avert the death order that threatened him. Now there would be other recipients.

The only thing left for him was to punish those responsible for this "blood-letting", and to take his blood back in the same way. So he too issued a "death order" addressed to his mother, his sisters and his wife.

In the analysand's fantasy life, the role of issuer of the death order and that of its recipient were at times reversed, at others confused, and sometimes they even became identical.

What brought him into analysis was when he found himself face to face with the "death order" that he had been carrying around within him and had suppressed all the previous years. Awakening came when his aging mother became ill and asked for his help. The analysand was forced to have her come and live with him because his sisters refused to give her any help whatsoever.

He was obliged to assume increased financial burdens. At the same time, his co-habitation with his mother brought back his childhood years. He re-lived all his past, including its emotional charge, moment by moment. He inevitably encountered the "death order" that his parents had issued for him; he was frightened and became confused; his anxiety and his mental tension kept growing.

He wanted to transform the issuers of the "death order" into recipients. His inclination was to throw his mother out, and to beat up his sisters. His friends, seeing him in this condition, urged him to seek the help of a specialist.

In my first meeting with him, I found myself sitting in front of a heavy, 45-year-old man, very anxious, angry and in a state of obvious confusion and disorganisation. He talked ceaselessly when describing the above facts related to his life.

In the sessions that followed, he asked for the analyst's help in confronting his inner world but also the reality of his bed-ridden mother. He stated: "*My house has been transformed into a hospital. I sleep on the couch. I have given my bedroom to my mother ... I feel very close to death, as though I were going to die tomorrow. It is a feeling I have had ever since I can remember. I dream that my mother and my wife are together and I am jealous. I will go crazy.*" In this way he informed me how he would feel if his female psychoanalyst became an ally of his mother's and his wife's. He calls his inner world a "treasure", the only thing he has in his possession.

The analysand has taken to wandering the streets again, in order to avoid contact with his mother who sets his internal inclinations in motion.

t is, I believe, important to note that when he talks about "blood-letting unto death", he believes that this "blood-letting" will take place and that it will kill him. It is obvious to the analyst that, in his particular psychic state, he is unable to function on a symbolic level. After some time in analysis with me, his inner terror was gradually reduced and he was able to find the best possible solution with regard to his mother. Eventually the positive feelings of love and concern for her came to the surface, thus confirming Melanie Klein's view that "*Where there is hate there is love.*"

In conclusion, it can be said that the "death order" for the analysand was the financial blood-letting, and his inability to resist it. The analysand did not face this death order until he reached the age of 45.

Regarding transference, it has become evident that, for the analysand, the Analyst-Analysand-Relationship is one of "Blood-letting". This is confirmed by the fact that, the analysand has all along being using various pretexts to delay paying the Analyst. For him this signifies that he would rather be the issuer of the "Death order" than its recipient. It would seem, that "blood-letting" is the prototype relationship for the analysand, the only one he has experienced. As a result he can do nothing other, than repeat it with me -his analyst-.

This is the history of "the death order" to date. It is hoped, however that psychoanalysis will be able to help the analysand to sublimate his intense feelings and above all those related to "death order which has proved to be a part of his psychological state.

This case is recorded because of its inevitable difficulties in terms of countertransference and therapeutic technique

References

Baudelaire, C.P. (1857), Fleurs du Mal.

Bion, W.R. (1957), Differentiation of the psychotic from non-psychotic personalities, Int. Journal of Psychoanalysis, 38.

Bion, W.R. (1970), Attention and interpretation, in Seven Servants: Four Works by Wilfred R. Bion, New York: Aronson, 1977.

Freud, S. (1900), The Interpretation of Dreams, S.E. 4-5.

--- (1920), Beyond the pleasure principle, S.E. 18.

--- (1940), An outline of psychoanalysis, S.E. 23.

Klein, Melanie (1939), The importance of symbol formation in the development of the ego in Klein (1975, ibid.)

--- (1975), The writings of Melanie Klein Vol. I, Love, Guilt and Reparation and Other Works, 1921-45, Vol. II.

Segal, Hanna (1978), On symbolism, Int. Journal of Psycho-Analysis, 59.

C

DISCUSSION

Discussion

Psychoanalysis never ceases to challenge analysts. We analysts are searching for the unknown - the unconscious of our analysands, since we believe that this is necessary in order to practise our profession effectively.

The question is: when, how and under what circumstances is the unknown unconscious delivered to us - if ever. Experience has taught us that the unconscious is well hidden, protected and not communicable owing to the analysand's building up of defensive systems.

I do not pretend to have the answers to these questions. However, I will endeavour to formulate my thoughts on the subject. I have deliberately selected these particular cases from my practice in order to challenge analysts and allied professionals further and hopefully to shed more light on their understanding.

Let us start with the analysands who did not deliver their inner world because they did not trust the analyst. Sometimes, however, they inform the analyst of its existence. I would cite as an example here an analysand who had been in analysis with me for ten years when he came to a session one day and said: "*All these years I have kept my paranoid delirium for myself alone. I have kept notes about it. Today I brought them in to give to you.*" He took a sheaf of notes out of his pocket and showed them to me, saying: "*Here is my delirium and I will give them to you,*" and then put them back into his pocket. And of course he left my office taking his secret world with him. His analysis continued despite this event, because I felt it would benefit him.

Another analysand of mine, some years after the termination of his analysis, approached me at a social event and showed me a file of poems that he had written during his years of analysis with me, saying that he would give them to me. However, after we chatted for a while, he left taking the file full of his poems with him.

Anna, after she discontinued her analysis with me she send me the following poems which she wrote during her analytical period but kept them secret.

HOPKINS, AND OTHERS OF MY PAST, FREUD HAS YOU BEAT TO HELL

It's all prepared ......
    I'll have the operation.

There are scars on my eyes
and in my head.
The doctor said
my vision was impaired,
and that my visionings.

        And though I thought it well till now,
        my sight is speckled
        (who knows how?)
        and he said only surgery
        would change the dappled world I see
        to represent reality.

                If shadows of old memories
                blacked out the light,
                they have shown other views more bright,
                and intricate patterns dazzle me.
                Design has been my first delight.

        But I've hidden my kaleidoscope
        (the doctor called it "distancing");
        I'm losing fantasy's relation,
        Forgetting the game of associations.

The doctor says that I can hope
to find, when he restores my vision,
a soothing slant of checkerboard precision ...
and learn to deal with clear-cut blacks and whites.

THE BIGGEST CONFECTIONERY IN THE WORLD

Getting them back in shape
is your job, eh,
Dr. A.?
Well, state your preference:
isn't so far off the track.

    (To get me back in shape is
    up to you. Your decision).

And you haven't met with so much opposition,
unless this absolute liability could be
termed resistance or hostility.

Well I'm not fighting now.
I' m just surprised at how you say the shape will hold
from day to day when I am better - organized.

"One mold,
but any size or color".
You display that
    (there are big ones
    and small ones
    there are blue ones
    there are yellow ones).

The cardinal grace that they are all marshmallow ones.
The essence of a well-adjusted state, they take a brief
impression but they never lose their shape.

When,
old patterns dying hard, it seems impossible to spar
the call-controlling past, one contrast yet remains.
Before I go to far, one phrase to say ...
The 'permanent set' is either way.
Lost I Forget.

In these particular cases, I let them do their own thing without commenting or putting pressure on them to deliver to me what they wanted to keep for themselves. I let them play the cat-mouse game with me, having adopted this technique as a product of my experience with these particular individuals.

"Beyond psychoanalysis" was the title that came to my mind when I sat down to write on the cases presented in this paper. I believe that training in psychoanalysis and a great deal of experience contributes greatly to understanding, handling and helping these individuals.

Whether we like it or not, they often come to analysts, on whom they exert pressure to accept them for analysis. They demand that the analyst help them to understand themselves better and eventually to enjoy life and relationships in particular. The latter are their Waterloo. Hence they inform the analyst that his endeavour is not going to be easy or uneventful, as is evident from the clinical material presented above. It goes without saying that this work has its limitations since these analysands are in ongoing analysis.

What we have learned from them so far is that, in spite of the fact that they hide their inner world, they must be aware to some degree of what they carry deep in their soul, because they build up strong barriers of defensive systems to ensure their psychic survival and to avoid threatening breakdowns. However, during the psychoanalytic process, we learn that they have experienced mini-breakdowns which they were able to overcome in their own "way", e.g. by acting out, small deceptions, abrupt actions in their life, promiscuity, homosexual experiences, battering relatives or friends, etc.

Acting in is frequent, testing the analyst's honesty and above all attempting to control the analyst and make him fail in his profession, etc. Underneath there is a feeling of despair, a plea for help which comes across to the analyst, but which the analysand is frequently unaware of.

It seems to me that if the analyst is capable of containing these individuals, who are difficult in many ways, and of containing the outbreak of their inner world, then the analysands can do the same, i.e. to contain themselves more adequately. As a result, their internal threat is reduced. I risk stating that in such individuals there is an urge sooner or later to act out and deliver their inner world, no matter how dangerous it might be. They are often seeking some external event to trigger such an occasion.

It is the analyst who is taken by surprise when facing the outbreak of their inner world even when he suspects that there is a hidden part of their soul. From there on it is easier for both analysand and analyst to continue. They have become allies working towards the common goal of increasing the analysands' capacity to enjoy life and relationships.

Developmentally speaking they have entered the depressed phase bringing with them strong elements from the paranoid phase, and therefore did not manage to complete the depressed phase. The delivery of their inner world to the analyst will enable them to pass into the depressed phase well enough. The question remains of how long it will take them to attain this purpose. This to some extent explains why these individuals remain so long in analysis.

As an example, I would like to cite the following material. In the case entitled "*Testimony*", *I could not avoid asking the analysand to explain the fact that he delivered his inner world to his analyst in the 30th year of his analysis. He answered: "As a philanthropic act to myself. I let my inner world - the fever of murder - come out slowly and in instalments. It would have been intolerable to me to break out suddenly. I would not have been able to handle it.*"

Sure enough, he hints that the analyst should adopt a philanthropic technique in dealing with him.

We must keep in mind that these analysands intend to create a symbiotic relationship with the analyst, which they seem to enjoy. Sooner or later they will go through the depressed phase sufficiently well. The time needed for this process is usually fairly long and varies from one individual to another, depending on several factors that are not relevant to this paper. There are also analysands who remain in analysis even though they mistrust the analyst and establish with him a pseudo-symbiotic relationship as a reference point regarding relationships; the possibilities of a satisfactory analytical outcome are limited in these cases. However, experience has taught us that if the analyst succeeds in meeting the unconscious of the analysand and in working slowly and safely through the paranoid elements that are very strong in these cases, it is possible that he will enable the analysand to pass into the depressed position sufficiently well. It is understood that the containment of these individuals is necessary and favours the analytical process. Thus I have observed that when the analytic process is interrupted suddenly for external reasons deriving from the analysands, they regress. They return to their 'normal' state as soon as they resume their analysis.

It is hard to suggest the technique most suitable for these individuals. It seems to me that that the psychoanalytic technique remains the main tool. It sometimes needs to be modified, depending on the case at hand, i.e. attention should be paid to interpretations as far as timing and dosage are concerned, e.g. interpretations could also be given bit by bit until resistances are reduced. Also in some cases non-interpretation policy for some time has its advantages because it can overcome inhibitions and help to further the psychoanalytic process. The stability and credibility of the analyst are essential. Indeed a number of my analysands confided to me after completing their analysis that a more important role was played in their progress by the credibility of the analyst than by gaining insight through interpretations. To my mind, the above are useful in order to help the individuals who in the past were regarded as unsuitable for analysis.

D

Children and Adolescents in Danger

In the 1970s I joined the staff of the University Pediatric Hospital of Aghia Sophia when the director was Professor and Academician Nikolaos Matsaniotis. I worked as a child psychiatrist and analyst, and had to meet the needs of children and their families who came from all over Greece for advice on various psychological problems. In this capacity, I have seen the full spectrum of problems ranging from simple to severe ones.

I will cite two categories of cases that I found to be particularly interesting for a pediatric hospital. The first category had to do with various cases of children 6-14 who appeared to be psychotic, but were not. Their condition was due to severe negligence on the part of the parents who were unaware that their negligence could affect their children and jeopardise their psychological health.

From the history and the evaluation of these families, the following common characteristic emerged: the mothers were cooperative with me, the psychoanalyst; they were good-hearted people who meant well and cared for their families and for the child they brought in for advice. However they worked very hard not only in the house, taking care of their husband and the other children, but they also pitched in with the farm chores.

So the children were left in the "care" of numerous persons such as neighbours, relatives, etc., i.e. anybody available. As a result, these mothers neglected their children from all points of view, not because they did not love them, but because they were overburdened by work and unable to cope with their lives. After all, most of them had been brought up in the same way and had no idea this was not a good enough way to raise their children. As a result, their family life was chaotic. But when they realised that their children had deteriorated instead of progressing, i.e. they were failing at school, difficult to manage, unhappy, quarrelled with their siblings, had no friends, etc., these mothers rushed to the hospital to seek help. I decided to see the mothers and children by myself in a joint interview and individually as well, depending on the case. My approach and technique were motivated by the desire to do the best for the mother and child alike, and ultimately to improve them both.

So, since they were living far away from the hospital on islands, etc, I encouraged monthly appointments and followed them for a considerable period of time, until I believed that they could continue on their own, advising them that they could consult me whenever they felt the need. It is assumed that these children did well from then on, since the parents did not contact the hospital again in later years.

Considering the circumstances, I focused my work with them on the following important points: The stability of the household, the stability of the child's daily life, the importance of the presence of both parents to the family and especially that of the mother. I let them know that communication and interrelations favour family life.

Following the evaluation, I would see the mothers individually, giving them a chance to discuss any problems that preoccupied them, other than those related to the child they had brought for advice. Such problems included frustrations that had to do with their families, their marriage, etc. Regarding the children, I was seeing them individually, when play therapy and verbal or mixed techniques were applied, according to the child in question.

The children made contact easily with the analyst. They were confused about the role of their family members. Slowly they were helped to understand that their parents meant well but neglected them because they had difficulties meeting the needs of the family due to their work. Eventually their anxiety decreased and they appeared more relaxed. When their mothers and I found that they had progressed on all levels, it was decided to terminate our meetings for the time being.

It must be stressed that the positive outcome in these cases was based on the cooperation of these families with the therapist - myself - on all levels, and on the good, positive relations that were established between the parties concerned. I did not have a chance to meet the fathers because circumstances did not permit, since they had to work, as well as looking after the rest of the family while the mother and one child came to the hospital for their appointment.

This report indicates that severe negligence of children, even when due to the ignorance of the parents can endanger the children's psychological health.

The second case has to do with a regressed five-year-old boy who needed hospitalisation urgently. He had been found wandering the streets, he refused to speak, and was brought to the same hospital by the police. Upon admission, he was examined by the pediatrician, who found him healthy but very thin and dehydrated. He was apathetic, passive and refused to eat or speak. He was put on an IV and fed parenterally. He made no contact whatsoever with the hospital personnel. I was asked to see him and evaluate him from the psychological point of view. He did not respond to me either, despite all my efforts. So then I decided to sit next to him and talk to him. I explained to the boy that we were going to keep him in the hospital for some time to look after him and that we would try to find his parents. The boy was placed in a ward with other children who had various physical problems. His case was discussed with the pediatricians who were familiar with this type of problem. I shared with them my plan regarding his treatment as follows: I decided to assign a social worker exclusively for the boy. She was asked to sit next to his bed and try to establish verbal contact with him by offering him toys etc. but without pressuring him. As for myself, I saw him daily and talked to him throughout his stay in hospital. At the same time, we asked the police to look for his parents. Indeed, 3-4 days later, the police brought his mother to the hospital. Her appearance was very neglected and she was almost catatonic. We asked her to visit the boy every day, to talk to him, and stay with him until he was discharged, which she did.

Hence we now had two patients to take care of: mother and child. I used to see the mother individually every day with the intention of establishing a relationship with her and evaluating her psychological condition. She had been deserted by her husband and was living in an abandoned dilapidated house with her four children, the youngest of whom was our patient. This mother was cooperative but very ill psychiatrically, and therefore incapable of looking after either her family or herself. Home visits confirmed this fact. It is understood that the hospital took charge of all the children for further evaluation and treatment. The father was never located.

The boy began to speak and eat after about 15 days, but was

kept in hospital for two months until his physical and psychological condition was sufficiently improved.

My work with him continued in my office at the hospital after he was able to speak, eat by himself and move around. In the beginning, he was slow and hesitant, and preferred to play with the toys available; but he seemed to accept me. Eventually he improved. His facial expression became more lively and at times he would look at me, talk to me, and engage me in his play.

This boy's case was discussed with the hospital staff and we all agreed that since his mother was unable to look after her family, the boy should be placed in a nearby foster home and followed up closely by the hospital services.

It is understood that the social services took care of this family on all levels, financially, with home visits, evaluations of the other children, any treatment required, etc.

From the above it is evident that the team approach and a good follow-up programme are necessary for a positive outcome in such cases with multiple problems.

The following cases have been selected from my private practice.

A charming nine-year-old girl was brought to the author because, although she spoke at school, she had stopped speaking at home. She was an adopted child. Her parents meant well but were insecure in their role. Their main difficulty was that they kept her distanced from them because they were afraid of her, not knowing how to handle her. I was seeing the little girl on a weekly basis and encouraged her to continue her activities. For about three months she would sit in an armchair and fall asleep. I had to wake her up at the end of the session and bring her to the parent in the waiting room.

Slowly the girl began to be interested in the toys available. For about a month she played by herself, then she would involve the analyst in her play and later she began talking during play, using just a few words here and there.

It wasn't until six months later that she eventually addressed the analyst. From there on the results of the analytical work were visible. Until then, the analyst contained the girl's regression and applied a non-interpretation policy for some time in order to reduce the girl's resistance and inhibitions. She progressed slowly and her analysis was terminated after two years.

During her analysis, the main themes that emerged were around her adoption. She would see herself alone, living in a household with her adopted parents who gave her many things, but not enough warmth or love. She felt that they were good people, but somewhat awkward in their relationship with her. Also, she kept dreaming up various scenarios with regard to her biological parents, the most common of which was rejection by them.

She was reserved and quiet with the analyst, careful not to make any mistakes or break anything. Slowly she became less inhibited and made progress, becoming more and more like any other girl of her age.

Regarding the cause of her severe regression, it is difficult to say. It might have been due to several factors, such as the adoption per se. The lack of warmth on the part of the adopted parents, unknown biological parents and, last but not least, the constitutional sensitivity of the girl herself.

I was seeing the adopted parents together in monthly appointments. They spoke about their frustration at being unable to have their own children, about their difficulties in looking after a child who was a "stranger" to them. They were somewhat fearful of her, and felt they had failed in their role as parents.

The analyst supported them in their role, and gradually they became more relaxed. They were advised to contact the analyst in case of need, which they never did.

The following case concerns a five-year-old girl whose father asked for an appointment because his daughter was having nightmares and outbursts of rage that the parents were unable to handle; she also refused to go to school. The girl was brutalised by her older sister physically and emotionally.

In the first interview, she was brought in by her mother, who was holding the child in her arms as tightly as possible. They sat down. The girl was sucking her thumb and hid her face on her mother's breast. They looked like two children ready to burst into tears.

Any attempt on my part to enter into contact with the child resulted in violent temper tantrums, ending in exhaustion so that the child eventually fell asleep. The little girl was taken into individual analysis, and I was seeing the parents at the same time. For some time, I was seeing the mother and daughter together, until the mother was finally able to allow her child to be alone with the analyst.

At first the parents wanted to be seen separately because of the palpable hostility between them; they could not stand to be together. Much later they were seen in a joint interview, in which they blamed each other for their child's condition.

The mother, 29 years old, had been brought up in a boarding school because her parents were separated. She had suffered from deprivation, was openly rejected by her mother and also suffered sadistic treatment at the hands of her older sister. In other words, the mother was the second child in her own family, as was the 5-year-old girl whom she had brought to the analyst. The little girl was the narcissistic object for her mother (by identification). The mother identified with the little girl and not only rejected her but wanted to destroy her.

The mother was aware of her murderous impulses towards the child. She tried to control them by keeping the child close to her and not allowing her to go to school.

The mother confessed to the analyst that when the child was at school, her murderous impulses were stronger and almost overwhelmed her. It was then that she hoped the child would be killed by a car and never return home.

She said she did not want her child to have a better life than she had. In addition she permitted her older daughter to victimise the little girl as her own older sister had victimised her.

When the child woke up during the night screaming in terror at some nightmare, the mother refused to comfort her. The father could not stand the child's screaming and instead of comforting her, he became furious and bit her.

The father confessed to the analyst that he had a recurring

dream that "the girl was in a house and was killed by an attack of Arabs."

My work with the child was facilitated by the fact that both parents were in analysis individually. The girl remained in analysis until her symptoms subsided and she became independent and happy.

I could go on reporting numerous cases of children who were endangered either because their parents, although well-meaning, were overburdened with work and unable to care for their children or because they were psychologically ill themselves and unsuited to their role as parents. It is, however, beyond the scope of this paper to present additional cases of children in danger. I wanted here in particular to demonstrate the child-adult continuum and its relationship to the environment - family, school, hospital and psychiatric services.

It is understood that children and adolescents could also be in danger for reasons known or unknown to us, e.g. an autistic 4-year-old boy who never developed language is now 35 years old. He lives with his family and participates in several social activities. This is due mainly to his father who, over the years, learned to understand his son's strange communication - with different types of screams - and eventually to handle him. I have been following him all these years and intervene only when the son went through acute violent crises which would subside with the help of medication.

It goes without saying that he could have been exposed to various dangerous situations against himself or others were he not closely supervised by his family, and thus protected from his own violence.

The same conclusion could be drawn from the case of a 16-year-old adolescent psychotic with compulsive, obsessive defences. He was referred to me because he was unable to study during his last year of college. A good-looking intelligent adolescent in his first interview, forbade me to see his parents. I learned much later that he concealed from me, his analyst, his physical violence, when he would hit his nanny who lived with the family and had brought him up since birth. For this reason the young man did not want me to meet his parents. I accepted this condition. I saw him for eight months on a weekly basis. He was punctual in his appointments. During this time, he never addressed me directly.

Without discussing this with me in advance, he decided to start using the French language, which I accepted silently. His underlying anxiety did not escape my attention.

For a number of sessions, he talked about aeroplanes. He would describe the engine in detail and was obsessed with the vol d'appui and vol d'avance. When he finished with aeroplanes, he proceeded to the next theme which was about cars, in which he was obsessed with the piston. For myself, I was in the dark about his real life.

One day in June, he came in and announced to me that he had graduated with college with high honours. He looked happy and told me he was going to leave for France and London to look for a university at which to continue his studies. He added that he was aware that he would not be able to enter university in Athens, which was a fact.

He came back a few days later and stated that he had decided to go to a university in London, where he had already been accepted. He added that he would go ahead with his plans if I agreed.

This took me by surprise. It was the first time he had addressed me directly. I have to confess that I did not know what to do. Nevertheless I said: Since you wish to continue with your studies, you should go to London and I will refer you to an analyst there, which I did. He accepted.

We parted. Since then he has made no further contact with me. Whether I did the best I could for him is a question that still occupies my mind, i.e. whether I should have accepted his plans and referred him to another analyst, and what this meant for him.

One day three years later, his mother came to my office without an appointment. She was physically small, fearful and very polite. She brought me a gift, a silver ball filled with chocolates.

She said she wanted to meet me and thank me for the interest I had shown in her son. This was how I received news of this difficult adolescent who was by then nearly 20 years old. He was doing very well at the university in London, but was having a hard time with himself. He was having psychoanalytic treatment but exhibited violent outbursts both verbally and physically against his own family, especially his mother. For this reason, his analyst in London referred him to a psychiatrist who added medication which the young man accepted. The last news which I had was that after his graduation from university he found a job and remained in England.

Thus in order to protect this adolescent from danger - his own violence - it was necessary to mobilise several therapeutic methods, which we did.

Let us hope that he continues his life to his own satisfaction.

E

Summary

It should be pointed out that the cases presented in this paper were selected with a view to meeting one criterion, violence and its derivatives, and thus the same theme is found here as in the supervised cases.

The above clinical material indicates that when analysands are able to deliver their psychotic core to the analyst, the psychoanalytic process is facilitated. Greater attention should be given to analysing children. The danger is that the analyst will identify with the child against the parents or vice versa.

It is not my intention to suggest that seeing children and parents in parallel is the only possible method of treatment. But at that time there was no other psychiatrist in the hospital, so it was left to me to treat children and parents alike.

I share the view of other analysts that the knowledge deriving from the analysis of children contributes to the understanding of adults, especially when they go through regressive stages. Modification of the classical psychoanalytic technique might be necessary when one is dealing with cases such as those presented in this paper, whether they are adults or children.

Contact with the staff of a pediatric hospital is facilitated when the child's analyst is also a pediatrician, as am I.

From the above, it is evident that the prevention of psychological problems at all ages, in children, adults and families, is the key to avoiding more serious cases.

It is my hope that this monograph will add to the understanding of both the phenomena of supervision and the special cases presented here.

F

BIBLIOGRAPHY

1. Alexandris, A., 1997, Countertransference, Karnac Books.
2. Bion, W.R., 1957, Differentiation of the psychotic from the non-psychotic personalities, Int. J. of Psychoanalysis, 38.
3. --- 1963, Elements of Psychoanalysis, London Heineman.
4. --- 1977, Attention and Interpretation, New York Aronson.
5. Clarkin, John F., Phd, Yeomas, Frank, E.M.D., PhD., Kernberg, Otto, F.M.D. 2006, Psychotherapy for Borderline Personality, American Psychiatric Publishing, Inc.
6. Fleming, John, M.D., Benedek, F. Therese, M.D., 1982, Psychoanalytic Supervision, A method of Clinical Teaching. Classics in Psychoanalysis, Monograph No. 1, International University Press, Inc. New York, N.Y.
7. Freud, S., 1900. The interpretation of dreams, S.E., 4.5.
8. --- 1909b, Analysis of a phobia in a five-year-old boy, S.E. 10.
9. --- (1918 [1914]). From the history of an infantile neurosis. S.E., Vol. 17.
10. --- 1914b, On Narcissism, S.E. 14.
11. --- 1915a, Instincts and their Vicissitudes, S.E. 14.
12. --- 1915, The Unconscious, S.E. 14.
12. --- 1920, Beyond the Pleasure Principle, S.E. 18.
14. --- 1933, New Introductory Lectures on Psychoanalysis, S.E. 19.
15. Jacobson, E., 1971, Depression, New York, Int. Un. Press.
16. Kernberg, Otto, 1980, Internal and external reality, N.Y. Aronson.
17. --- 1982, Self, Ego, Affects and Drives. J. Amer. Psychoanal. Assn.
18. --- 1997, Aggression, Hatred and Social Violence, Canadian Journal of Psychoanalysis, V. 6, No. 2.
19. Klein, M., 1931, Psychoanalysis of children
20. --- 1921-1945, Love, Guilt and Reparation and other works.
21. --- 1946, Notes on some schizoid mechanisms.
22. --- 1948, On the Theory of Anxiety and Guilt. First published in I.J.Ps - A. XXIX.
23. ---, Riviere, J., Love, Guilt and Reparation. The Hogarth Press and the Institute of Psycho-Analysis, 1953, 58-68.
24. Mahler, M. 1968, On human Symbiosis and the vicissitudes of individuation. New York. Int. U. Press.

25. --- 1979, Selected Papers of M.S. Mahler, New York: Aronson.
26. Segal, Hanna, 1950. Some aspects of the analysis of a schizophrenic. Int. J. of Psycho-Analysis, 31.
27. ---. 1986, The work of Hanna Segal, London Free Association Books.
28. ---. 1991, The New Library of Psychoanalysis, 12. Ed. Elizabeth Bott-Spillius, Dream, Phantasy and Art.
29. Winnicott, D.W., 1958, Collected papers, Through Pediatrics to p-sychoanalysis, New York, Basic Books.
30. --- 1965, The Maturational process and the facilitating environ-ment. New York Int. Un. Press.